Thelwell's
Pony Cavalcade

Thelwell's
Pony Cavalcade

ANGELS ON HORSEBACK
A LEG AT EACH CORNER
RIDING ACADEMY

MANDARIN

A Mandarin Paperback
THELWELL'S PONY CAVALCADE

First published in Great Britain 1981
by Methuen London Ltd
This paperback edition first published 1986
Reissued in 1992
by Mandarin Paperbacks
an imprint of Reed Consumer Books Limited
Michelin House, 81 Fulham Road, London SW3 6RB
and Auckland, Melbourne, Singapore and Toronto

Reprinted 1993, 1994 (twice)

ISBN 0 7493 0388 3

A CIP catalogue record for this title
is available from the British Library

Printed and bound in Great Britain
by Cox & Wyman Ltd, Reading, Berks

ANGELS ON HORSEBACK

~AND ELSE~ WHERE

by
thelwell

For
DAVID & PENNY

Most of the pictures originally appeared in *Punch* and are published here by kind permission of the proprietors.

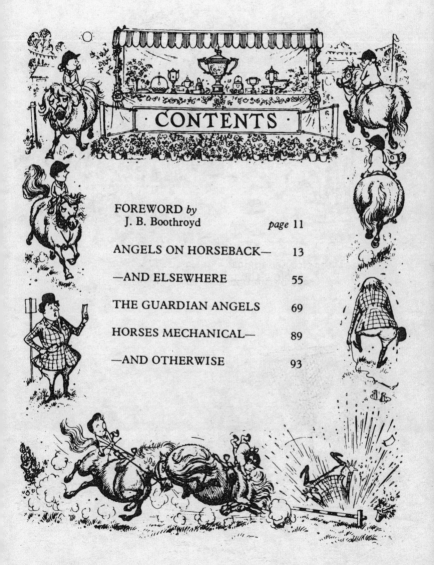

CONTENTS

" Now the fall is important."

FOREWORD

THERE was a song, 'Crazy Over Horses'. They weren't Thelwell's kind, but the kind that exist on shaved green turf for the few, the back page of the evening papers for the many—and for him nowhere. He doesn't recognize them. His horses never brought a grandstand to its feet, clashing binoculars. Brains are not blown out over them. Yet they are the horses that people who know horses know.

I do not know horses. But I have come nearer to it through these drawings than in any other way. For me they have humanized both horses and horsepeople—and if you think there is no such thing as a human horse, eavesdrop at the nearest Hunt Ball. As a lifelong non-equestrian I have suffered many a pang of inferiority, because there is something terribly crushing about anyone on a horse. Even a home-going labourer clomping past me in a country lane, side-saddle and bareback (if that can be), tempts me to touch my forelock, and astounds me by touching his first.

No doubt it's something to do with the height. The rider can't help looking down on the rest of the world, and it is easy to imagine that he is looking down his own nose as well as the horse's. However, I know at last that is not so. Thelwell has convinced me, and I can never be too grateful, that the horse person is, if possible, even less sure of himself than I am. Even those russet-coloured lumps on horses' backs that prove, as they jog into focus, to be small children in tiny velvet caps and impeccable little Jodhpurs which they must be literally growing out of every second, hold no terrors for me now. They are revealed as palpitating bundles of exposed nerve-ends, liable to be shot through a blackthorn hedge any minute like a stone from a catapult. This comforts me. In future, instead of avoiding the eye of middle-aged ladies with bowler hats and Roman noses who gallop at me round the blind corners of Sussex byways, I shall watch them keenly out of sight. Thelwell may have a disaster arranged for them.

Punch has had equestrian artists before. In mid-Victorian times it was difficult to open a copy without being trampled. But the creations between these present covers achieve something entirely new: they combine portraiture with caricature, a thing which most artists would hesitate to try with human beings, let alone the more temperamentally elusive and psychologically inscrutable horse. This means that while no horse could possibly look exactly like a Thelwell horse, all Thelwell horses manage to look exactly like horses. If anyone can explain this, or express it more lucidly, they should write to the publishers, please, not me.

To end with a reminder that Thelwell is not only an artist but a humorist is not to suggest that anyone could overlook it, but to make it clear that I haven't. It is hard for one practising humorist to praise another . . . but how is it that all these centuries have gone by without anyone thinking of the joke on page 51? Or 60? Or, for that matter ——?

But, anyway, they're all yours now.

J. B. Boothroyd

ANGELS ON HORSEBACK

Booted and Spurned
A GUIDE TO BRITISH PONY BREEDS

1. *DARTMOOR AND EXMOOR*
Though inclined to be wild—these ponies make lovable mounts if taken from the moors early enough.

2. *CONNEMARA*. Mostly grey nowadays—are among the oldest inhabitants of the British Isles.

3. *NEW FOREST*. Due to the abundance of traffic in the area—this rather narrow breed is said to be immune to the terror of modern roads.

4. *WELSH MOUNTAIN*
Perhaps the most beautiful of our native ponies but it is debatable whether the 'dished' face line is due to Arab influence.

5. *FELL AND DALE.* Originally used to carry lead—are ideal for the larger family.

6. *HIGHLAND.* The largest and strongest and quite unrivalled in surefootedness.

7. *SHETLAND.* The smallest and hardiest breed of all and perfect for introducing children to the problems of horsemanship.

" 'ow do *they* feel then? "

" I see you've kicked the toes out of them already."

Small in the Saddle

A FEW POINTERS WHEN BUYING A PONY

1. A child regards his first pony as a new plaything.

2. They must suit each other in temperament

3. Experience is needed when buying from public auctions

4. It is not always easy to recognise a good pony "in the rough".

5. The mount should not be too wide for the child's short legs.

6. Daily exercise is most important

7. And careful grooming
essential to the pony's happiness

Anyway, it's a wonderful way for a child to learn how
to enjoy Man's mastery over nature.

Look before you Leap
A CHILD'S GUIDE TO SHOW-JUMPING

A horse or pony is said to have " REFUSED " if
he stops in front of a fence . . .

. . . and to have " FALLEN " if the shoulders and
quarters have touched the ground.

Look before you Leap
A CHILD'S GUIDE TO SHOW-JUMPING

A competitor is eliminated for showing any fence to a horse after a refusal.

Or for unauthorised assistance whether solicited or not.

Look before you Leap
A CHILD'S GUIDE TO SHOW-JUMPING

Endless patience is required to reach perfection.

But for those who ultimately achieve a clear round—the rewards
are many.

Horse Show
AT THE WHITE CITY

Miss Pam Smith on the famous " Tusker " enters the arena.

Willowbrook Show
ON THE GREEN

Shirley Wilkinson and " Tearaway " enter the ring.

Horse Show
AT THE WHITE CITY

Mr. Robinson's " Firebird " taking the water.

Willowbrook Show
ON THE GREEN

Tom Jenkins' " Thistledown " taking the water.

Horse Show
AT THE WHITE CITY

Col. Boyce-Partington on " Prince Consort " at the wall.

Willowbrook Show
ON THE GREEN

Four-year-old Penelope Bright riding " Nimble "
tackles an obstacle.

Horse Show
AT THE WHITE CITY

The Marquis of Basingstoke presented the trophies.

Willowbrook Show
ON THE GREEN

" Well jumped Mary ", laughed Mrs. Hornby-James
who presented the prizes.

WILLOWBROOK
RIDING SCHOOL

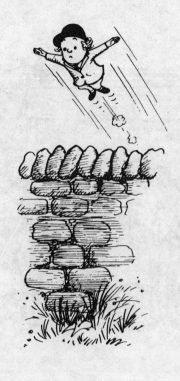

JUDGES' TABLE

" I'm sorry I ever mentioned he'd got a stone in his hoof."

"HEEL!"

–And Elsewhere

" What have I told you about drawing on the walls? "

" You rang? "

"... and hurry ..."

The Guardian Angels

70

" Charles! Did you ask anyone to meet you here this morning? "

" Increasing mechanisation of the countryside is enabling
more and more people to afford the luxury of owning . . . .

. . . a horse."

" Just *look* at it! ' Lacks initiative . .
Easily dominated . . .' "

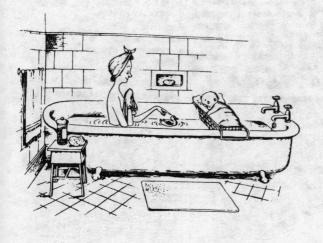

83

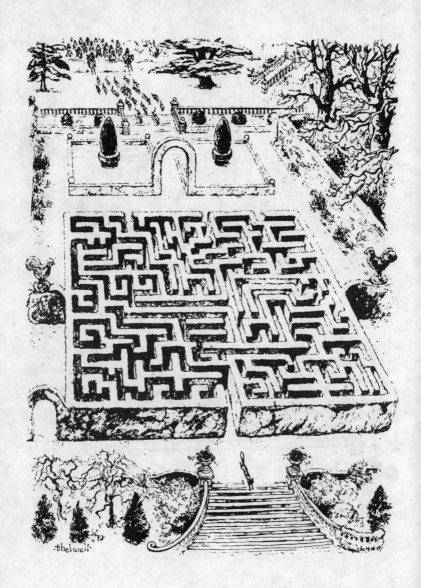

" Same again George."

HORSES MECHANICAL

– AND OTHERWISE

" Pretty-pretty."

" Give Fred a shout as you go by—he's doing the traffic census."

A LEG
AT EACH
CORNER

thelwell's

COMPLETE
GUIDE TO
EQUITATION

**FOR
PENELOPE**

This drawing reproduced by permission of the Proprietors of *Punch*

CONTENTS

How to Get a Pony

Acquiring a pony is not quite as easy as it sounds . . .

It is against the law to take them from the New Forest

– and risky to buy them from public auctions.

So look out for one which a friend has grown out of –

or buy one from
someone you trust.

When choosing . . .

good feet are most important

– and good manners
essential

– the eyes will tell you more
than any other feature . . .

but expert advice is needed as defects are often covered up.

Some ponies do not move well –

some do not move at all.

You will learn a great deal from a glance
at his teeth and remember –

never buy a horse that whistles.

You won't find your perfect
pony straight away –
but sooner or later . . .

. . . he'll find you.

LEARNING TO RIDE

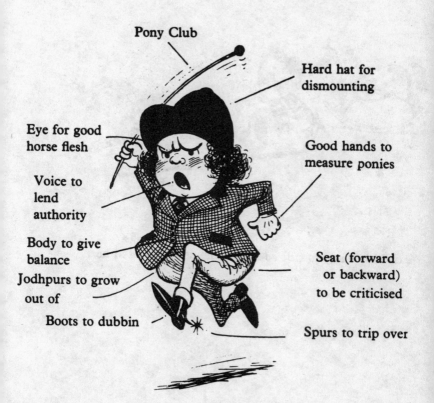

Pony Club

Hard hat for dismounting

Eye for good horse flesh

Good hands to measure ponies

Voice to lend authority

Body to give balance

Seat (forward or backward) to be criticised

Jodhpurs to grow out of

Boots to dubbin

Spurs to trip over

POINTS OF A RIDER

A child is ready to ride as soon as he shows himself keen ...

but it is inadvisable to influence him against his will.

The method of mounting is not important ...

. . . so long as it is safe.

The correct sitting position must be mastered

and exercises carried out in the saddle –

The natural aids to horsemanship are the hands, the legs, the body and the voice –

The artificial aids . . .

are whips, spurs, martingales
and gags.

Grip will improve with experience

and balance
with practice –

Talk to your pony – he will know what you mean –

and spend as much time in his
company as you possibly can.

* * * * * * *

In spite of our
constant criticism
of children today

there is no doubt
that they have . . .

as much spirit of adventure – determination . . .

. . . and downright courage . . .

. . . as their parents . . .

. . . ever had.

GROOMING

Make sure your pony is securely tied.

You will know when his coat needs attention –

– but don't clip him yourself unless
you are an expert.

Begin grooming by removing all surplus mud –

– and tone up his muscles by banging with a sack of wet straw.

Use the body brush vigorously – he will enjoy it.

Polish his coat with a rubber.

Get his tail well into the bucket when shampooing –

But beware of washing the mane
just before a show.

Detergents should be avoided

and tail-pulling undertaken with care.

Finish off by applying bandages to the legs.

SCHOOLING

A happy pony thinks of you as his best friend

so never lose your temper over some little mistake

but have some tit-bit handy when he does well.

He must be taught to stand correctly –

– to be led without fuss

144

and to move off promptly, when ordered to do so.

He will quickly get used to having his bridle put on –

but you should put smaller weights on his back before
attempting to mount him yourself.

Mastery is achieved by subtlety . . .

. . . not by abuse

but at least two people may be necessary to work
him on the lunge rein.

Ponies are natural jumpers

but don't expect miracles too early.

Endless patience is required –

and absolute authority must be maintained.

Once you have gained your pony's respect
half the battle is won.

HEALTH

Warble — Thrush

Humour
Sweet Itch
Colic

Strangles
Girth Gall
Saddle Sore

Splint

A FEW COMMON AILMENTS

If bored, ponies develop troublesome vices . . .

. . . so try to keep him entertained.

If simple ailments are detected –

don't panic

make him warm and comfortable

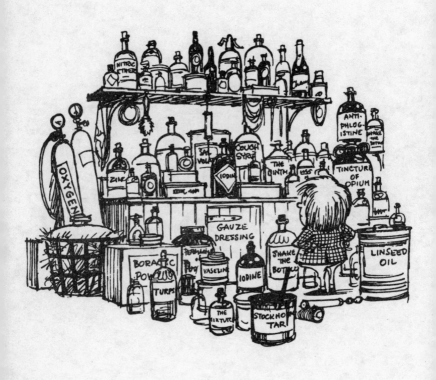

keep a few simple remedies handy

and learn how to administer them.

Colds can be relieved by inhaling eucalyptus –

and coughs by smearing the back
of the tongue with paste.

If he is constantly trying to scratch himself,
suspect skin trouble

and if he rolls about, it is probably colic.

Sympathetic nursing can work wonders –

but don't try to replace the vet.

You will know it has all been worth it
when he's up and about again.

BREEDS

The NEW FOREST pony lives almost exclusively on a diet of lettuce, cucumber and fish-paste sandwiches.

Owing to the harshness of its environment the
DARTMOOR has become tough and hardy.

The **EXMOOR** is mealy-mouthed.

The WELSH MOUNTAIN – our most beautiful
native breed – is inclined to be a trifle
wide in the barrel.

The ancient CONNEMARA was hanging
about Galway Bay long before the
song-writers got there.

FELL AND DALE can carry prodigious weights with ease.

The HIGHLAND is used
by sportsmen to carry
their 'bag' down the
mountains.

The SHETLAND – which is the world's
smallest breed . . .

. . . is respected by all who know horse flesh.

There are other ponies too – known as
BLOOD PONIES.

They can be seen in action at horse shows
all over the country.

SHOW JUMPING

Competitors must enter the arena mounted.

They may adopt the forward seat . . .

. . . or the backward seat

but they must not start until the signal is given . . .

. . . or stop before completing the course.

No more than three refusals are permitted –

and no foot must touch the water.

Blinkers are not allowed –

and unauthorised assistance is prohibited.

Don't expect to win every time . . .

. . . your turn will come.

＊　　＊　　＊　　＊　　＊

HOW TO TIME YOUR JUMPS

Take-off
too early
◀

Take-off
too late
◀

Take-off just right

There is no doubt at all in the
minds of horse lovers . . .

that the long hours of patient training . . .

. . . laborious work . . .

. . . careful grooming . . .

. . . are amply repaid . . .

. . . by the thrill of attending . . .

. . . a gymkhana.

HUNTING

Nose for 'owning' the scent

Head for 'Throwing up'

'Stern' for 'feathering'

'Voice' to 'give tongue'

A HALF COUPLE OF HOUNDS

Scent

Brush

Mask

'CHARLES JAMES' OR 'THE VARMINT'

A smart turnout is of first importance.

See that your pony arrives at the meet quite fresh.

Don't wait until the secretary
asks before you pay your 'cap' –

and give the master a polite greeting when you see him.

The fox is frequently referred to by other names –

but a hound is a hound and must never be called
anything else.

Always do exactly what the huntsman tells you . . .

and if you must talk in the field – make it a whisper.

Don't monopolise the best fences –

and even if you're able to keep up with the hounds . . .

you're not a real rider until you've been blooded.

POINTS TO REMEMBER

An untidy rider is an insult to a horse.

Do nothing which may cause him alarm –

but he should be introduced
to the hazards of modern
traffic.

An active pony will need shoeing regularly.

Keep something handy to pick out his hooves.

Make sure that his tack fits snugly – or it may chafe

and always check the girth before you move off.

Don't jump fences too close to trees –

– or leave gates open after going through them.

Keep a sharp lookout for signs of lice –

and if he's a kicker you must tie a red ribbon on his tail.

When you win something – don't take all the credit yourself . . .

... remember who did most of the work.

Don't keep him out when he wants to go home

and always attend to his comfort before your own.

In short – treat your pony as you like
to be treated yourself.

FOR
DAVID

CONTENTS

'Remember what I told you, girls,
never let him see you're afraid.'

THE MOUNT

'Do you have one like this in dapple grey?'

Some children discover the joys of
riding at a very early age . . .

. . . others prefer to wait until they are bigger.

Once in the saddle, however, they
are all reluctant to leave it.

Finding a reliable pony is not easy –

professional advice should be sought . . .

Finding a reliable professional
can also have its snags.

You must bear in mind that fat ponies can be hard on the legs . . .

and thin ones hard on the jodhpurs.

Young animals can be unpredictable

and old ones just the reverse.

Some instinct will tell you whether you are going to get on well together.

But *never* buy the first one you see . . .

. . . some day you may want to sell him.

If you buy a pony that is difficult to catch – take plenty of lump sugar with you

and eat as much of it as you can . . .

You will need all the energy you can get.

You may learn a great deal
about a pony by looking
at his teeth

This often applies also . . .

. . . to the rider.

FIRST PRINCIPLES

'No! No! Deirdre, you've got the wrong foot in that stirrup.'

Most children make very rapid strides as soon as they get into the saddle.

Although steady progress is less easy to maintain –

Mutual respect must be established between pony and rider.

But it should be clearly understood who's boss.

Never speak angrily to your pony.

Use a kind, gentle voice.

It will be just as effective.

Never use spurs –

Do not expect him to be able to read your mind.

Show him exactly what you would like him to do . . .

He'll be very happy to oblige you.

Ponies are very well known for their courage.

But they can be shy, sensitive creatures . . .

So if any obstacle should cause him trouble . . .

. . . take him back . . .

. . . reassure him . . .

. . . and make him do it again.

THE ACADEMY

'Hand up the one who spotted my deliberate mistake.'

Always get up early when going to riding school – you'll need plenty of time . . .

. . . to waken your pony.

Don't dawdle on the way . . .

Don't try to be clever . . .

Always enter a riding school by the front gate.

Make friends with the other children.

You will learn a lot from them.

Just sitting on a pony's back is not riding –

so work hard at your studies . . .

There will be plenty of time for play.

Most instructors enjoy a joke . . .

but don't go too far –

Expulsions are difficult for all concerned.

CARE OF YOUR PONY

'Don't just sit there, dear – hurry home before he catches a chill.'

It is unkind to ride your pony too fast –

Insufficient exercise, however,
can lead to excessive fat.

So give him a good lively trot every day.

The result will astonish you.

Neglecting your pony's coat
is a serious matter . . .

. . . which cannot fail . . .

. . . to cause trouble.

If flies bother him in hot weather . . .

tie a sprig of elder to his brow band . . .

he will find it a great relief.

Your pony's shoes should be checked regularly . . .

Neglect of this simple precaution . . .

can lead to sore feet.

You must learn to recognise signs
that your pony is off colour –

Roaring may indicate wind troubles . . .

. . . and kicking may mean a sore spot . . .

You will know when it's time to call for the vet.

SAFETY PRECAUTIONS

'What have you done with her *this* time?'

Make sure you know how to pick up his foot . . .

Lack of ability in this direction

may cause you inconvenience.

Never shout 'Gee up'

. . . when teacher is mounting.

Always examine fences carefully
before jumping.

This will enable you to be ready . . .

for any emergency.

Never try out novel ways of
getting into the saddle . . .

you'll enjoy quite enough variety –

– getting out of it.

If accidents are likely to occur . . .

. . . avoid worry . . .

. . . by making sure that there is a qualified vet in attendance.

Remember that the rules of the road apply to you . . .

as well as to other road users.

All road signs must
be strictly obeyed

and all hand signals
correctly given.

Some riders like to have a lot of
bandages on their horses.

This is not always as pointless . . .

. . . as it may appear.

WHAT TO WEAR

'I'm breaking in a new pair of boots.'

A smart turnout is
extremely important . . .

A rider's ability can usually be judged

from her appearance.

There is no point in being well
groomed yourself, however,

unless you are prepared to make your pony . . .

. . . look the same.

Roomy jodhpurs are advisable . . .

and a hard hat is a must . . .

Elaborate whips impress nobody – but remember . . .

the most essential item

in a rider's wardrobe

is a good pair of boots.

GOOD MANNERS

'Don't be so mean, Georgina –
let Christabel have a turn.'

Never let your pony nip other peoples' . . .

It is bad manners for one thing . . .

and can lead to painful results.

The judge's decision must always be accepted as final.

Do not blame your instructor . . .

... every time something goes wrong.

Don't play with your pony in the garden –

or allow him into the house.

Don't make fun of other people . . .

. . . you may not be perfect yourself.

You must not expect your mother to keep your pony clean

or your father to give him exercise.

Never forget that winning prizes is not everything . . .

Those who make the odd blunder . . .

are often more popular.

ACADEMY PICTURES

'You have to approach her slowly and quietly . . .

'. . . holding out a lollipop.'

'It's just a question of which she breaks first, the pony or her neck.'

'You're wasting your time, darlings – you can lead them to the water . . .

... but you can't make them drink.'

'Putting shoes on for you lot is playing old Harry with my eyesight.'

'Next year you can go
pony trekking on your own.'

'They know perfectly well they're supposed to drink
lemonade as a stirrup cup.'

'That was mean – telling her you're engaged to David
Broom.'

'He can manage on tinned food. Why can't you?'

'If I lay my hands on those perishing kids . . .'

'How many trading stamps did
they give you with him?'

'I wish you wouldn't keep hiding them in
your bedroom. We'll have the whole house
overrun with hounds again.'

'I'm sorry, Mrs Chadwick,
but when your daughter fell
at the double oxer,
I'm afraid she broke a leg.'

A Selected List of Fiction Available from Mandarin

While every effort is made to keep prices low, it is sometimes necessary to increase prices at short notice. Mandarin Paperbacks reserves the right to show new retail prices on covers which may differ from those previously advertised in the text or elsewhere.

The prices shown below were correct at the time of going to press.

☐	7493 1352 8	**The Queen and I**	Sue Townsend	£4.99
☐	7493 0540 1	**The Liar**	Stephen Fry	£4.99
☐	7493 1132 0	**Arrivals and Departures**	Lesley Thomas	£4.99
☐	7493 0381 6	**Loves and Journeys of Revolving Jones**	Leslie Thomas	£4.99
☐	7493 0942 3	**Silence of the Lambs**	Thomas Harris	£4.99
☐	7493 0946 6	**The Godfather**	Mario Puzo	£4.99
☐	7493 1561 X	**Fear of Flying**	Erica Jong	£4.99
☐	7493 1221 1	**The Power of One**	Bryce Courtney	£4.99
☐	7493 0576 2	**Tandia**	Bryce Courtney	£5.99
☐	7493 0563 0	**Kill the Lights**	Simon Williams	£4.99
☐	7493 1319 6	**Air and Angels**	Susan Hill	£4.99
☐	7493 1477 X	**The Name of the Rose**	Umberto Eco	£4.99
☐	7493 0896 6	**The Stand-in**	Deborah Moggach	£4.99
☐	7493 0581 9	**Daddy's Girls**	Zoe Fairbairns	£4.99

All these books are available at your bookshop or newsagent, or can be ordered direct from the address below. Just tick the titles you want and fill in the form below.

Cash Sales Department, PO Box 5, Rushden, Northants NN10 6YX.
Fax: 0933 410321 : Phone 0933 410511.

Please send cheque, payable to 'Reed Book Services Ltd.', or postal order for purchase price quoted and allow the following for postage and packing:

£1.00 for the first book, 50p for the second; **FREE POSTAGE AND PACKING FOR THREE BOOKS OR MORE PER ORDER.**

NAME (Block letters) ....

ADDRESS ....

....

☐ I enclose my remittance for ....

☐ I wish to pay by Access/Visa Card Number ☐☐☐☐☐☐☐☐☐☐☐☐☐☐☐☐

Expiry Date ☐☐☐☐

Signature ....

Please quote our reference: MAND